5 STEP ENGLISH
The Gift of the Magi

5단계로 술술 읽히는 영어원서
단계 영어 크리스마 선물

초   판 | 1쇄 발행 2025년 10월 20일

지 은 이 | 오헨리
영어번역 | 신자경, 스티브오
그   림 | M.J 화이트
정보맵핑 | 이야기 연구소
디 자 인 | 박소연
제 작 처 | 다온피앤피
특허등록 | 10-2717987호
국제출원 | PCT/KE202/002551

펴 낸 곳 | ㈜도서출판동행
펴 낸 이 | 오승근
출판등록 | 2020년 3월 20일 제2020-000005호
주   소 | 부산광역시 부산진구 동천로 109, 9층
이 메 일 | withyou@withyoubooks.com
카카오톡 | @도서출판동행

단계별 요약정보 기술은 국내특허등록 및 PCT 국제출원을 했습니다.

이 책은 저작권법에 따라 보호받는 저작물이므로 무단 전재와 복제를 금지하며,
이 책 내용의 전부 또는 일부를 이용하려면 반드시 출판사의 서면 동의를 받아야 합니다.
잘못된 책은 구입하신 서점에서 바꿔 드립니다.

ISBN 979-11-91648-54-6(13740)

5단계로 술술 읽히는 영어원서

단계영어

크리스마스 선물

머리말
Prologue

언어 실력이 자라날수록,
영어책도 함께 자라야 합니다.

성인이라면 더 이상 성장할 여지가 없다고 생각하기 쉽지만, 언어 학습은 다릅니다. 옷이나 신발은 이미 딱 맞더라도, 새로운 언어를 배울 땐 '한 치수 큰 사이즈'를 준비해두는 편이 좋습니다. 왜냐하면 우리의 학습 능력과 사고력은 나이를 불문하고 계속해서 발전할 수 있기 때문이죠. 언어 실력이 자라날수록, 우리가 접하는 영어책도 함께 '진화'해야 합니다.

어린 나뭇가지를 예로 들어볼까요? 그냥 두면 이리저리 휘지만, 조기에 올바른 지지를 해주면 곧게 자랍니다. 성인 학습도 마찬가지입니다. 매번 새 자료를 무작정 시작하기보다, 이미 배운 내용을 조금씩 확장해 나가는 것이 훨씬 효율적이니까요. 이 책은 하나의 스토리를 단계별로 심화하여 5단계로 발전시킨 신개념 영어 도서입니다.

언어 능력이 자라나는 과정을 생각해 보면, 처음에는 간단한 표현부터 시작합니다. 그러다가 점차 말이 길어지고, 내용이 풍부해지죠. 예컨대 "밥 먹고 싶다"에서 "오늘은 내가 좋아하는 음식으로 식사를 하고 싶다"로 자연스레 확장되는 것처럼, 표현 방식은 달라져도 '배가 고파 음식을 원한다'는 핵심은 그대로입니다.

이 책의 5단계 구성은 바로 이런 원리를 바탕으로 만들어졌습니다. 전하고자 하는 메시지는 동일하지만, 그 표현 범위와 깊이는 단계가 올라갈수록 점차 넓어지도록 설계되었죠. 독자 여러분께서는 한 계단씩 오르듯 각 단계를 학습하면서, 자기만의 속도와 수준에 맞춰 영어 실력을 발전시키는 즐거움을 누리게 되실 것입니다.

여러분의 영어와 사고력을 함께 '키우는' 새로운 경험, 지금부터 시작해보시기 바랍니다.

스티브 오

It's easy to assume that as adults, we don't have much room left to grow. But language learning is a completely different story. Even if your clothes and shoes fit perfectly, when you're starting a new language, it's often better to "go up a size." Our ability to learn and think can keep developing, no matter our age. And as our language skills improve, the English books we use should also "evolve" accordingly.

Imagine a young tree branch: if it's left unattended, it may grow crooked. But if you support it properly from the start, it will grow straight. Adult learning works in much the same way. Instead of constantly searching for entirely new materials, it's often more effective to build on what you already know, expanding your knowledge step by step. This principle is at the heart of this book—a fresh approach to English learning that develops a single story over five progressive stages.

Think about how our language abilities naturally grow. We begin with basic phrases, and over time, our expressions become more detailed. For instance, "I want to eat" might evolve into "I'd love to have my favorite meal today," yet the core message—"I'm hungry, and I want to eat"—remains the same.

The five-stage structure in this book is based on that very idea. While the central message stays consistent, each stage broadens and deepens the way it's conveyed. As you climb through the levels at your own pace, you'll discover the joy of steadily enhancing your English skills.

Let this mark the beginning of a whole new experience where both your English and your critical thinking can continue to grow. Take the first step and see how far you can go!

Steve Oh

사용설명서
Manual

단계 영어
오디오북 채널

영어는 언어입니다. 영어는 암기보단, **실제 사용을 통해 익혀야 합니다.** 즉, 의미가 있어야 하고 내가 사용해야 합니다. 이 책은 학습자가 아닌 책으로서 영어를 의미있게 사용할 수 있게 제작했습니다.

간단하지만 명확하게 도서 사용방법을 말씀드리겠습니다.

❶ 영어 공부가 아닌 **책을 읽는다고 생각하세요.**

❷ **레벨 1부터 읽으세요.** 레벨1이 무척 쉽게보여도 일단 레벨 1부터 읽어야 다음 단계로 수월하게 올라갈 수 있습니다. 마치 계단을 오를 때, 첫 계단에 발을 내디디고 그 다음 계단으로 오르는 것처럼 말입니다.

❸ 모르는 단어가 보이면 **사전을 찾지 마세요.** 다시 한번 말씀드리지만 이건 책입니다. 책은 읽어야 합니다. 우리가 보통 책을 읽을 때 국어사전을 찾으면서 읽지않는 것처럼 말입니다.

❹ **레벨 5까지 읽었다면 이제 레벨 4, 3 순으로 거꾸로 읽어보세요.** 복잡한 문장들이 어떻게 간략하게 요약되는지를 배울 수 있게 됩니다.

사용법은 위 4가지면 충분합니다.
자, 그럼 이제 시작해 볼까요?

---

1) 레벨5에서는 사전을 찾으셔도 됩니다. 내용 이해를 위해서가 아닌 모르는 단어의 정확한 의미 파악을 위해 사전을 찾을 필요가 있습니다.

Audio Book
Channel

English is a language, Language should be learned through practical use rather than memorization. That means, it has to make sense and you have to use it. This book is not a study book, but a book designed to use English in a meaningful way.

I will tell you how to use the book in a simple but clear way.

❶ Do not think that you study English. Instead, read the book.

❷ Read the book from level 1. Even if level 1 looks very easy, you should read level 1 first to move up to the next level with ease. It's just like climbing the stairs. When you go upstairs, you place your foot on the first stair and then go up to the next one.

❸ If you see word you don't know, don't consult a Dictionary. a Again, this is a book. The book must be read. It's just like we don't consult an English dictionary when we usually read an English book.

❹ If you have read all the way to level 5, now read books backwards in order of level 4 and 3. You will learn how to concisely summarize complex sentences.

If you have learned above 4 methods, it is sufficient.
So, let's get started, shall we?

목 차
Contents

단계 영어
오디오북 채널

머리말

독자 후기

도서 사용법

The Gift of the Magi **LEVEL 1** 18

Chapter 1	One Dollar Eighty-Seven Cents	20
Chapter 2	Della's Hair	22
Chapter 3	Jim's Present	24
Chapter 4	Della's Waiting	26
Chapter 5	Jim Sees Della's Hair	28
Chapter 6	The Set of Combs	30
Chapter 7	Christmas Presents	32

The Gift of the Magi **LEVEL 2** 34

Chapter 1	One Dollar Eighty-Seven Cents	36
Chapter 2	Della's Hair	40
Chapter 3	Jim's Present	44
Chapter 4	Della's Waiting	48
Chapter 5	Jim Sees Della's Hair	52
Chapter 6	The Set of Combs	56
Chapter 7	Christmas Presents	58

The Gift of the Magi **LEVEL 3**   62

Chapter 1	One Dollar Eighty-Seven Cents	64
Chapter 2	Della's Hair	68
Chapter 3	Jim's Present	70
Chapter 4	Della's Waiting	72
Chapter 5	Jim Sees Della's Hair	74
Chapter 6	The Set of Combs	76
Chapter 7	Christmas Presents	78

The Gift of the Magi **LEVEL 4**   82

Chapter 1	One Dollar Eighty-Seven Cents	84
Chapter 2	Della's Hair	88
Chapter 3	Jim's Present	92
Chapter 4	Della's Waiting	96
Chapter 5	Jim Sees Della's Hair	100
Chapter 6	The Set of Combs	104
Chapter 7	Christmas Presents	108

The Gift of the Magi **LEVEL 5**   112

Chapter 1	One Dollar Eighty-Seven Cents	114
Chapter 2	Della's Hair	118
Chapter 3	Jim's Present	122
Chapter 4	Della's Waiting	124
Chapter 5	Jim Sees Della's Hair	126
Chapter 6	The Set of Combs	130
Chapter 7	Christmas Presents	132

단계영어
크리스마스 선물

LEVEL 1

단어(Words)

440개

LOW　　　　　MIDDLE　　　　　HIGH

문장수(Sentences)

68개

LOW　　　　　MIDDLE　　　　　HIGH

문장길이(Sentence Length)

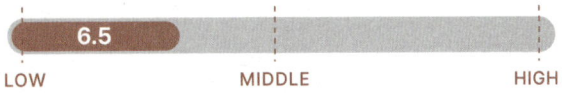

6.5

LOW　　　　　MIDDLE　　　　　HIGH

읽는 시간(Reading time)

1분 45초

LOW　　　　　MIDDLE　　　　　HIGH

말하는 시간(Speaking Time)

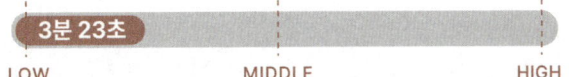

3분 23초

LOW　　　　　MIDDLE　　　　　HIGH

LEVEL 1

Chapter 1 - One Dollar Eighty-Seven Cents

It was the day before Christmas. Della had $1.87. It was not enough to buy a gift.

Della sat in a chair and cried. Her home was very old.

There was a name on the door. The name was "Mr. James Dillingham Young." Della was his wife, and she called him "Jim."

The next day would be Christmas. She wanted to buy a present for Jim, but she only had $1.87.

Chapter 2 - Della's Hair

A tall, narrow mirror stood in the living room. She stood in front of the mirror. She looked at her hair and let it down.

Jim and Della had two precious things. Jim had a gold watch. Della had beautiful hair.

Della's hair was very long. It shone and touched her knees. She cried quietly.

She put on her jacket, then went out to the street.

Chapter 3 - Jim's Present

She went to a hair shop and sold her hair. She got $20.

She looked for Jim's present. Finally, she found it. It was a white gold watch chain. Jim had an old chain, so it was the best for him. She paid $21 and then went back home.

Chapter 4 - Della's Waiting

She sat down and styled her hair. It took forty minutes to curl it. "He will say I look like a chorus girl," she thought.

She made coffee and got ready to cook. She heard his footsteps and then prayed. "Please, God, let me look pretty."

Chapter 5 - Jim Sees Della's Hair

The door opened, and Jim looked at Della. He stopped in surprise.

She came closer to him and said, "Jim, I sold my hair.
I wanted to buy you a nice gift.
Merry Christmas, Jim!"

"You cut off your hair? Really?" he asked.

"Yes, you can see it's gone," she replied. "Anyway, may I put the meat in the pan now, Jim?"

Chapter 6 - The Set of Combs

Suddenly, Jim put a gift on the table. He hugged Della.
"Della, I still love you. I was just surprised."

She opened the small box and cried. There were special combs in the box.

Della really wanted them. But now, her hair was gone. She cried and hugged them.

Chapter 7 - Christmas Presents

Then, she gave him the watch chain. "It's perfect for you," she said.

Jim smiled. "Actually, I sold the watch to buy those combs. Let's put our gifts aside and enjoy dinner together!"

In the Bible, three wise men gave gifts to baby Jesus. That is how Christmas gifts began.

Now, Della and Jim are wise like them. They are the wisest.

단계영어
크리스마스 선물

LEVEL 2

단어(Words)

607개

LOW   MIDDLE   HIGH

문장수(Sentences)

80개

LOW   MIDDLE   HIGH

문장길이(Sentence Length)

7.6

LOW   MIDDLE   HIGH

읽는 시간(Reading time)

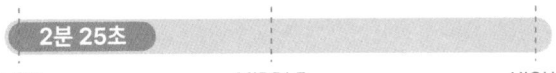

2분 25초

LOW   MIDDLE   HIGH

말하는 시간(Speaking Time)

4분 40초

LOW   MIDDLE   HIGH

LEVEL 2

Chapter 1 - One Dollar Eighty-Seven Cents

Christmas was the next day. But Della had only one dollar and eighty-seven cents. It wasn't enough money to buy a present.

Della sat on the sofa and cried. Her home was old and modest; the weekly rent was eight dollars.

In front of the door, there was a letterbox. On the door, there was a card that read "Mr. James Dillingham Young." Della, his wife, simply called him "Jim."

Suddenly, she decided to have the best Christmas Day. She wanted to buy Jim a special present, but she had only $1.87. She needed a clever idea.

Chapter 2 - Della's Hair

Between the windows, there was a tall, narrow mirror. Suddenly, Della saw herself standing in front of it.

Della had especially long hair. Jim had inherited a gold watch from his grandfather. Both items were very important to them.

Della let her hair down, seeing herself in the mirror. Her hair was amazingly long and shiny. It fell down to her knees.

Tears fell onto the red carpet. After putting on her old jacket, she went outside.

Chapter 3 - Jim's Present

Della stopped in front of a hair salon. "Will you buy my hair?" she asked. She sold her hair and received twenty dollars.

She began looking for a gift for Jim. At last, she found the perfect gift: a shiny white gold watch chain. It was the best choice for Jim because he had an old chain. She paid twenty-one dollars. Now she had only eighty-seven cents. Holding the gift close, she hurried home to surprise him.

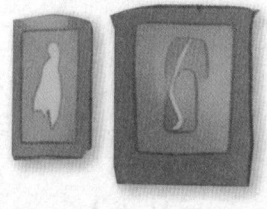

Chapter 4 - Della's Waiting

She took a deep breath and curled her hair with a curling iron. Soon, her hair was covered in tiny curls. She looked in the mirror for a long time. "Maybe he'll say I look like a dancer at an amusement park," she thought, "but I still think I did the right thing."

At seven o'clock, the coffee was ready, and the frying pan was hot. When she heard him walking up the stairs, she whispered, "Please, God, let me still look pretty to him."

Chapter 5 - Jim Sees Della's Hair

Jim opened the door and walked in. He looked exhausted. He paused when he saw Della.

She went to Jim and said, "Jim, please don't look at me like that. I cut my hair and sold it. It's Christmas, right? I needed a present for you. Merry Christmas, Jim!"

"You really did it?" Jim asked. He tried to understand.

"Yes," Della replied. "Please be kind to me. You know how much I love you. Anyway, may I begin cooking the meat now, Jim?"

Chapter 6 - The Set of Combs

Jim took a present and put it on the table. "Listen, Della," he said, "I will always love you. But I'm so surprised by what I bought."

Della opened it and began to cry. Inside were the special combs she always wanted, but now her hair was gone.

She hugged the combs and said, "It's okay! I can use them later!"

단계영어 크리스마스 선물 | LEVEL 2

Chapter 7 - Christmas Presents

Della then showed him her present. It was a beautiful watch chain. "I'm sure it will look good on you," she said.

Jim just smiled. "Della, let's keep them safe now. I don't have my watch anymore. I sold it to buy these combs. Well, how about we enjoy dinner together?"

In the Bible, there were three wise men. We call them the Magi. They were wise men because they brought gifts to baby Jesus. That's how Christmas gifts began. Now, Della and Jim are the wisest of all. They are the Magi.

단계영어

⟨ 크리스마스 선물 ⟩

LEVEL 3

단어(Words)

1175개

LOW　　　　　　MIDDLE　　　　　　HIGH

문장수(Sentences)

119개

LOW　　　　　　MIDDLE　　　　　　HIGH

문장길이(Sentence Length)

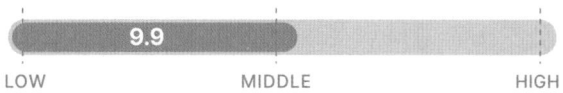

9.9

LOW　　　　　　MIDDLE　　　　　　HIGH

읽는 시간(Reading time)

4분 42초

LOW　　　　　　MIDDLE　　　　　　HIGH

말하는 시간(Speaking Time)

9분 2초

LOW　　　　　　MIDDLE　　　　　　HIGH

LEVEL 3

Chapter 1 - One Dollar Eighty-Seven Cents

Della had only one dollar and eighty-seven cents. It wasn't enough to buy a present. Whenever she went shopping, she asked shopkeepers for discounts. She managed to save sixty cents that way, but they were just small coins. None of the shopkeepers welcomed her because she always asked for discounts. Those sixty cents were her shame and tears. The next day was Christmas.

Della had nothing to do, so she cried a lot while sitting on the old sofa. Her home was very old and filled with worn furniture. There was a letterbox

in front of the door and an electric button, which was broken. There was also a card on the door that read "Mr. James Dillingham Young." He used to earn thirty dollars per week, but now he earns only twenty. He was poorer than before, but whenever he came home, his wife hugged him gently. Della was his wife, and she called him "Jim."

She looked out the window. Everything seemed gray to her. Tomorrow was Christmas Day. She hoped to buy a present for Jim, but she had only one dollar and eighty-seven cents. She collected every coin she could, but that was all. Still, she planned something nice for him.

Chapter 2 - Della's Hair

The room had a long, narrow mirror between the windows. It was not easy to see her full reflection. However, she was so thin that she could see herself. Suddenly, she turned around from the window and stood before the mirror. Quickly, she pulled down her hair and let it fall.

Della and Jim were proud of two things. One was Jim's gold watch from his grandfather. The other was Della's hair. If the queen of Sheba were alive, she would be jealous of Della's hair. Even King Solomon would envy Jim's watch because it was so impressive.

Della's hair was so long and shiny. It reached below her knees and shone like a waterfall. Tears fell from her eyes onto the red carpet. Then she put on her old brown jacket and old brown hat. Her eyes were still teary, but they glowed as she went out to the street.

Chapter 3 - Jim's Present

She went to a hair goods shop. "Will you buy my hair?" asked Della.
"I buy hair," said Madame. "Take your hat off. Let's have a look at your hair." Della let down her hair, which looked like a brown waterfall. She sold it and received twenty dollars.

She looked around different shops to find Jim's present. Finally, she found something that seemed made just for him: a white gold watch chain. It was perfect for Jim because his old chain was worn out. She paid twenty-one dollars, leaving her with only eighty-seven cents, and then she went back home to meet him.

Chapter 4 - Della's Waiting

As soon as Della got back home, she relaxed. She took out her curling irons to fix her shortened hair. It was not an easy job. In just forty minutes, her hair was covered with small, closely packed curls that made her look like a schoolboy. She gazed at her reflection in the mirror for a long time, checking it carefully.

"Jim might say I look like someone from Coney Island, with its flashy style," she thought, "but there was no other way with just one dollar and eighty-seven cents."

It was nearing dinnertime. The coffee was ready, and the frying pan was hot on the back of the stove, all set to cook the meat. Della sat at the table near the door where he always came in. Jim was usually punctual. She heard his steps on the stairs and worried for a moment. She often whispered small prayers for everyday concerns, and now she quietly said, "Please, God, I hope I still look pretty to Jim."

Chapter 5 - Jim Sees Della's Hair

Jim came in, opening the door. He looked a bit thin and serious. He was only twenty-two years old and had a wife to support. He needed a warm coat but didn't even have gloves. Standing by the door, he looked at Della with an expression she couldn't figure out. It made her uneasy. It wasn't anger or surprise, just something strange in his eyes as he stared at her.

Della approached him. "Jim," she cried, "don't look so surprised. As you see, I had my hair cut and sold it because I couldn't face Christmas without a present. It'll grow back quickly, and you won't mind, right? Merry Christmas, Jim! I got a wonderful present for you."

"Seriously? You mean, you cut your hair?" Jim asked, as if he still couldn't believe it.

"See, my long hair is gone," Della said. "Do you still like me, even without my hair? It's Christmas Eve! Please be good to me. I did it for you," she added sweetly. "No one can measure how much I love you. Shall I put the meat on the pan, Jim?"

Chapter 6 - The Set of Combs

Jim began to speak. "Don't get me wrong, Della," he said. "I love you no matter how you look. But if you open that package, you'll see why I was so surprised."

He took a small package from his coat pocket and set it on the table. She started unwrapping it and suddenly let out a sharp cry. Seeing the gift made her sob, and Jim had to comfort her at once.

Inside were the special combs Della had long admired in a Broadway store window. They were shiny, made of a special shell, with sparkly edges—perfect for her once-long hair. She had really wanted them, even though she never dreamed she could own them.

Now they were hers, but her lovely hair was gone. Holding them close, she looked up with teary eyes and smiled. "My hair grows really fast, Jim!"

Chapter 7 - Christmas Presents

Della suddenly stood up and looked surprised—like a kitten. "Oh, you haven't seen the lovely present yet!" she exclaimed. She was excited and finally handed it to him. The precious white chain sparkled like her eyes and reflected her joyful spirit.

"It's wonderful, right? It was not easy to find it, Jim. I'm sure the white chain is so fine that you'll want to keep checking the time every moment." Hearing that, he just lay down on the couch and smiled.

"Della," he said, "I love it so much but forget about it for now. I sold my watch because I needed money for your combs. Let's have a great Christmas Eve dinner!"

The magi were very wise men. They brought gifts to the Baby Jesus in the manger and started the tradition of giving presents at Christmas. Their gifts were probably very wise ones, maybe even ones you could exchange if needed. Now, I've told you about two people who sold their most precious things for each other. But let me tell you, in today's world, they were the wisest givers of all. They were like the magi.

단계영어
크리스마스 선물

LEVEL 4

단어(Words)

1796개

LOW　　　　　MIDDLE　　　　　HIGH

문장수(Sentences)

157개

LOW　　　　　MIDDLE　　　　　HIGH

문장길이(Sentence Length)

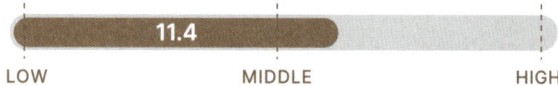

11.4

LOW　　　　　MIDDLE　　　　　HIGH

읽는 시간(Reading time)

7분 11초

LOW　　　　　MIDDLE　　　　　HIGH

말하는 시간(Speaking Time)

13분 48초

LOW　　　　　MIDDLE　　　　　HIGH

LEVEL 4

Chapter 1 - One Dollar Eighty-Seven Cents

Della had one dollar and eighty-seven cents. That was all. And sixty cents of it was in small coins (pennies). Della saved a dollar or two at a time by negotiating discounts with the owners of the grocery, vegetable, and meat stores. Her cheeks turned red with silent self-reproach. Della counted it three times, but she still had one dollar and eighty-seven cents. And the next day was Christmas.

There was clearly nothing to do but collapse on the old couch and scream. So Della did just that. Life is made up of tears, sadness, and smiles, with plenty of crying.

While Della gradually calmed down, let's take a look at the home. It was an eight-dollar-per-week apartment with basic furniture included. It wasn't completely beyond description, but it definitely caught the attention of those looking for people who needed help.

In the entrance below was a letterbox into which no letter would fit, and an electric button that no finger could press. Along with

that, there was a card that said "Mr. James Dillingham Young."

The name "Dillingham" had flourished when its owner was earning thirty dollars per week. Now, with the income reduced to twenty, they were seriously considering shortening it to a humble "D." But whenever Mr. James Dillingham Young came home, his wife called him "Jim" and warmly hugged him. His wife was Della, whom I've already mentioned. And that's all quite good.

Della stopped crying and reapplied her makeup. She watched a gray cat walking along a gray fence in a gray backyard through the window. Tomorrow was Christmas Day, and she had only $1.87 to buy Jim a present. She had saved every coin she could for months, but this was the best she could manage. It was impossible on twenty dollars a week. Expenses were higher than she had anticipated. She had only $1.87 to buy a present for Jim. For a long time, she had been planning something nice for him. She wanted something worthy of Jim.

Chapter 2 - Della's Hair

There was a narrow mirror between the windows. You may have seen something similar in an eight-dollar apartment. A very slim person might quickly get a fairly accurate view of their appearance. Della was skinny, so she had mastered this skill.

Suddenly, she turned away from the window and stood in front of the mirror. Her eyes were shining brightly, but then her face turned pale. Quickly, she let her hair fall to its full length.

Now, there were two things that James Dillingham Young truly cherished. One was Jim's old watch, which had belonged to his father and grandfather. The other was Della's long hair. If a queen lived in the building across the way, Della would have let her hair down one day just to flaunt it, and it might have made the queen feel less special. If a king worked as the building's caretaker, Jim would wear his watch every time he passed by, just to stir up envy in the man.

So now Della's beautiful hair flooded around her, waving and gleaming like a brown waterfall. It reached below her knees, like a dress. Then she nervously and swiftly pinned it back up. She paused for a moment, standing still, and shed a tear or two on the worn red carpet.

She put on her old brown jacket and her old brown hat. With a swish of her skirt and the same bright twinkle in her eyes, she flitted out the door and down the stairs to the street.

Chapter 3 - Jim's Present

She stopped where the sign read: "Ms. Sofronie. All Kinds of Hair Goods." Della hurried upstairs and exhaled. Madame—large, excessively pale, and cold—didn't look like a "Sofronie."

"Do you buy hair?" Della asked.
"Yes," said Madame. "Take off your hat and let me examine it."
The brown wave fell down.
"It's twenty dollars," said Madame, lifting the hair with a skilled hand.
"Give it to me quickly," said Della.

Oh, and the next two hours flew by like a breeze. She was searching stores for Jim's present.

Finally, she found it. It seemed as though it had been crafted specifically for Jim. There wasn't another one like it in any shop, and she had looked everywhere. It was a simple white gold chain, its value evident from the quality rather than any flashy decoration—as all good things should be. It was perfectly suited to his watch. The moment she laid eyes on it, she knew it belonged to Jim. Serene and valuable—both descriptions fit perfectly. They charged her twenty-one dollars, and she hurried home with the remaining eighty-seven cents. With that chain on his watch, Jim could check the time freely anywhere. As much as he cherished the watch, he sometimes looked at it secretly, aware of the worn leather strap he used instead of a proper chain.

Chapter 4 - Della's Waiting

When Della arrived back home, her excitement turned to caution. She retrieved her curling irons, lit the gas, and tried to fix the damage caused by her love-driven decision. It was a daunting task.

In less than an hour, her hair was full of small, tight curls, giving her the appearance of a mischievous schoolboy. She studied herself

in the mirror for a long time, examining every detail carefully.

"If Jim doesn't get really mad at me," she thought, "he might say I look like a dancer from Coney Island when he sees me. But what else could I do with only a dollar and eighty-seven cents?"

At seven o'clock, the coffee was ready, and the frying pan sat on the back of the stove, hot and ready for the chops.

Jim was always punctual. Della held the chain in her hand and perched on the edge of the table near the door he usually came through. Then she heard his footsteps on the stairs, faintly audible from the first floor, and she turned pale for a moment. She often whispered small prayers for everyday matters, and now she quietly said, "Please, God, let him still think I'm pretty."

단계영어 크리스마스 선물 | LEVEL 4

Chapter 5 - Jim Sees Della's Hair

The door opened, and Jim came in, shutting it behind him. He looked thin and very grave. Poor fellow—at only twenty-two, he already had the responsibility of supporting a family! He needed a new coat and had no gloves.

Jim stood by the door, unmoving, like a hunting dog catching the scent of a bird. He looked at Della with an expression she couldn't decipher, and it frightened her. It wasn't anger, surprise, disapproval, or horror, or any of the things she had expected. He simply stared at her with that peculiar look. Della slid off the table and approached him.

"Jim, my dear," she said, "please don't look at me like that. I cut and sold my hair because

I couldn't face Christmas without giving you a present. It will grow back—please don't mind, will you? I had no choice. My hair grows fast. Say 'Merry Christmas!' Jim, and I'll be happy. Guess what a lovely, beautiful gift I have for you."

"Did you cut your hair?" Jim asked slowly, as if he still couldn't believe it, even after thinking it over.

"I cut it and sold it," Della replied. "You still love me just the same, don't you? I'm still me,

even without my hair, right?" Jim glanced around the room in a curious way.

"Your hair is gone?" he said, sounding almost bewildered.

"You don't need to look for it," said Della. "I really sold it, I promise—sold and gone. It's Christmas Eve, darling. Please be kind to me, because I did it for you. Maybe someone could count the hairs on my head," she added sweetly, "but no one could measure my love for you. Shall I put the chops on now, Jim?"

Chapter 6 - The Set of Combs

Let's turn our attention to something less significant for a moment. Eight dollars a week or a million a year—what's the big difference? A clever person or a witty one might give you the wrong answer. The three wise men in the Bible brought valuable gifts, but they weren't necessarily perfect gifts. We'll understand this puzzling statement better later.

Jim took a package from his coat pocket and placed it on the table.

"Don't get me wrong, Della," he said. "I do love you, no matter what haircut or style you have. But when you open that package, you'll see why I was momentarily puzzled."

Her pale fingers quickly tore at the string and paper. First came a gleeful exclamation, followed—unfortunately—by an abrupt shift to uncontrollable tears, which required immediate comfort from Jim.

Inside were the combs that Della had admired for so long in a Broadway shop window. They were crafted from genuine tortoise shell, with jeweled edges. They perfectly matched her lovely, now-vanished hair. She knew they were expensive, and she had desired them even though she never dared hope to own them. And now they were hers, but the hair that should have been adorned by these precious accessories was gone.

She held them close, and after a while, she looked up with tearful eyes and smiled. "My hair grows really fast, Jim!"

Chapter 7 - The Christmas Presents

Then Della jumped up like an eager little cat and cried, "Oh, oh!"

Della hadn't yet shown him his wonderful gift. She took it out and set it on her open palm. The simple but precious metal sparkled, reflecting her excited and passionate spirit.

"Isn't it wonderful, Jim? I scoured every place to find it. You'll want to check the time a hundred times a day now. Give me your watch—I want to see how it looks." Instead of doing so, Jim sank onto the couch, placed his hands behind his head, and smiled.

"Della," he said, "let's put our Christmas

presents away for now and keep them safe. They're a bit too special to use at this moment. I sold my watch to get the money for your combs. So how about you start cooking the chops?"

The wise men, who were very clever, gave gifts to the baby in the manger, beginning the tradition of Christmas presents. As they were wise, their gifts were likely thoughtful. Perhaps they even allowed for exchanges if someone else brought the same gift. Here, I've told you the simple story of two foolish young people in a tiny apartment who selflessly gave up their greatest treasures for each other. But let me affirm, to all the wise of today, that of all who give gifts, these two were the wisest. Of all who exchange gifts, they are the wisest everywhere. They are the Magi.

단계영어
크리스마스 선물

LEVEL 5

단어(Words)

2090개

LOW　　　　　MIDDLE　　　　　HIGH

문장수(Sentences)

165개

LOW　　　　　MIDDLE　　　　　HIGH

문장길이(Sentence Length)

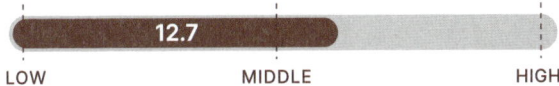

12.7

LOW　　　　　MIDDLE　　　　　HIGH

읽는 시간(Reading time)

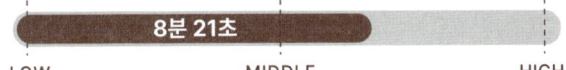

8분 21초

LOW　　　　　MIDDLE　　　　　HIGH

말하는 시간(Speaking Time)

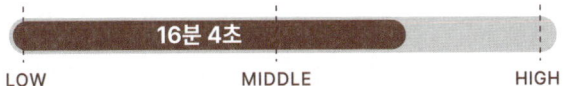

16분 4초

LOW　　　　　MIDDLE　　　　　HIGH

THE ORIGINAL TEXT

Chapter 1 - One Dollar Eighty-Seven Cents

One dollar and eighty-seven cents. That was all. And sixty cents of it was in pennies. Pennies saved one and two at a time by bulldozing the grocer and the vegetable man and the butcher until one's cheeks burned with the silent imputation of parsimony that such close dealing implied. Three times Della counted it. One dollar and eighty-seven cents. And the next day would be Christmas.

There was clearly nothing to do but flop down on the shabby little couch and howl. So Della did it. Which instigates the moral reflection that life is made up of sobs, sniffles, and smiles, with sniffles predominating.

While the mistress of the home is gradually subsiding from the first stage to the second, take a look at the home. A furnished flat at $8 per week. It did not exactly beggar description, but it certainly had that word on the lookout for the mendicancy squad.

In the vestibule below was a letter-box into which no letter would go, and an electric button from which no mortal finger could coax a ring. Also appertaining thereunto was a card bearing the name "Mr. James Dillingham Young."

The "Dillingham" had been flung to the breeze during a former period of prosperity when its possessor was being paid $30 per week. Now, when the income was shrunk to $20, though, they were thinking seriously of contracting to a modest and unassuming D. But whenever Mr. James Dillingham Young came home and reached his flat above he was called "Jim" and greatly hugged by Mrs. James Dillingham Young, already introduced to you as Della. Which is all very good.

Della finished her cry and attended to her cheeks with the powder rag. She stood by the window and looked out dully at a gray cat walking a gray fence in a gray backyard. Tomorrow would be Christmas Day, and she had only $1.87 with which to buy Jim a present. She had been saving every penny she could for months, with this result. Twenty dollars a week doesn't go far. Expenses had been greater than she had calculated. They always are. Only $1.87 to buy a present for Jim. Her Jim. Many a happy hour she had spent planning for something nice for him.

Something fine and rare and sterling—something just a little bit near to being worthy of the honor of being owned by Jim.

Chapter 2 - Della's Hair

There was a pier-glass between the windows of the room. Perhaps you have seen a pier-glass in an $8 flat. A very thin and very agile person may, by observing his reflection in a rapid sequence of longitudinal strips, obtain a fairly accurate conception of his looks. Della, being slender, had mastered the art.

Suddenly she whirled from the window and stood before the glass. Her eyes were shining brilliantly, but her face had lost its color within twenty seconds. Rapidly she pulled down her hair and let it fall to its full length.

Now, there were two possessions of the James Dillingham Youngs in which they both took a mighty pride. One was Jim's gold watch that had been his father's and his grandfather's. The other was Della's hair. Had the queen of Sheba lived in the flat across the airshaft, Della would have let her hair hang out the window some day to dry just to depreciate Her Majesty's jewels and gifts. Had King Solomon been the janitor, with all his treasures piled up in the basement, Jim would have pulled out his watch every time he passed, just to see him pluck at his beard from envy.

So now Della's beautiful hair fell about her rippling and shining like a cascade of brown waters. It reached below her knee and made itself almost a garment for her. And then she did it up again nervously and quickly. Once she faltered for a minute and stood still while a tear or two splashed on the worn red carpet.

On went her old brown jacket; on went her old brown hat. With a whirl of skirts and with the brilliant sparkle still in her eyes, she fluttered out the door and down the stairs to the street.

Chapter 3 - Jim's Present

Where she stopped the sign read: "Mme. Sofronie. Hair Goods of All Kinds." One flight up Della ran, and collected herself, panting. Madame, large, too white, chilly, hardly looked the "Sofronie."

"Will you buy my hair?" asked Della.
"I buy hair," said Madame. "Take yer hat off and let's have a sight at the looks of it."
Down rippled the brown cascade.
"Twenty dollars," said Madame, lifting the mass with a practised hand.
"Give it to me quick," said Della.

Oh, and the next two hours tripped by on rosy wings. Forget the hashed metaphor. She was ransacking the stores for Jim's present.

She found it at last. It surely had been made for Jim and no one else. There was no other like it in any of the stores, and she had turned all of them inside out. It was a platinum fob chain, simple and chaste in design, properly proclaiming its value by substance alone and not by meretricious ornamentation—as all good things should do. It was even worthy of The Watch. As soon as she saw it she knew that it must be Jim's. It was like him. Quietness and value—the description applied to both. Twenty-one dollars they took from her for it, and she hurried home with the 87 cents. With that chain on his watch Jim might be properly anxious about the time in any company. Grand as the watch was, he sometimes looked at it on the sly on account of the old leather strap that he used in place of a chain.

Chapter 4 - Della's Waiting

When Della reached home her intoxication gave way a little to prudence and reason. She got out her curling irons and lighted the gas and went to work repairing the ravages made by generosity added to love. Which is always a tremendous task, dear friends—a mammoth task.

Within forty minutes her head was covered with tiny, close-lying curls that made her look wonderfully like a truant schoolboy. She looked at her reflection in the mirror long, carefully, and critically.

"If Jim doesn't kill me," she said to herself, "before he takes a second look at me, he'll say I look like a Coney Island chorus girl. But what could I do—oh! what could I do with a dollar and eighty-seven cents?"

At 7 o'clock the coffee was made and the frying-pan was on the back of the stove hot and ready to cook the chops.

Jim was never late. Della doubled the fob chain in her hand and sat on the corner of the table near the door that he always entered. Then she heard his step on the stair away down on the first flight, and she turned white for just a moment. She had a habit of saying a little silent prayer about the simplest everyday things, and now she whispered: "Please God, make him think I am still pretty."

Chapter 5 - Jim Sees Della's Hair

The door opened and Jim stepped in and closed it. He looked thin and very serious. Poor fellow, he was only twenty-two—and to be burdened with a family! He needed a new overcoat and he was without gloves.

Jim stopped inside the door, as immovable as a setter at the scent of quail. His eyes were fixed upon Della, and there was an expression in them that she could not read, and it terrified her. It was not anger, nor surprise, nor disapproval, nor horror, nor any of the sentiments that she had been prepared for. He simply stared at her fixedly with that peculiar expression on his face. Della wriggled off the table and went for him.

"Jim, darling," she cried, "don't look at me that way. I had my hair cut off and sold because I couldn't have lived through Christmas without giving you a present. It'll grow out again—you won't mind, will you? I just had to do it. My hair grows awfully fast. Say 'Merry Christmas!' Jim, and let's be happy. You don't know what a nice—what a beautiful, nice gift I've got for you."

"You've cut off your hair?" asked Jim, laboriously, as if he had not arrived at that patent fact yet even after the hardest mental labor.

"Cut it off and sold it," said Della. "Don't you like me just as well, anyhow? I'm me without my hair, ain't I?" Jim looked about the room curiously.

"You say your hair is gone?" he said, with an air almost of idiocy.

"You needn't look for it," said Della. "It's sold, I tell you—sold and gone, too. It's Christmas Eve, boy. Be good to me, for it went for you. Maybe the hairs of my head were numbered," she went on with sudden serious sweetness, "but nobody could ever count my love for you. Shall I put the chops on, Jim?" Out of his trance Jim seemed quickly to wake. He enfolded his Della.

Chapter 6 - The Set of Combs

For ten seconds let us regard with discreet scrutiny some inconsequential object in the other direction. Eight dollars a week or a million a year—what is the difference? A mathematician or a wit would give you the wrong answer. The magi brought valuable gifts, but that was not among them. This dark assertion will be illuminated later on.

Jim drew a package from his overcoat pocket and threw it upon the table.

"Don't make any mistake, Dell," he said, "about me. I don't think there's anything in the way of a haircut or a shave or a shampoo that could make me like my girl any less. But if you'll unwrap that package you may see why you had me going a while at first."

White fingers and nimble tore at the string and paper. And then an ecstatic scream of joy; and then, alas! a quick feminine change to hysterical tears and wails, necessitating the immediate employment of all the comforting powers of the lord of the flat.

For there lay The Combs—the set of combs, side and back, that Della had worshipped long in a Broadway window. Beautiful combs, pure tortoise shell, with jewelled rims—just the shade to wear in the beautiful vanished hair. They were expensive combs, she knew, and her heart had simply craved and yearned over them without the least hope of possession. And now, they were hers, but the tresses that should have adorned the coveted adornments were gone.

But she hugged them to her bosom, and at length she was able to look up with dim eyes and a smile and say: "My hair grows so fast, Jim!"

Chapter 7 - Christmas Presents

And then Della leaped up like a little singed cat and cried, "Oh, oh!"

Jim had not yet seen his beautiful present. She held it out to him eagerly upon her open palm. The dull precious metal seemed to flash with a reflection of her bright and ardent spirit.

"Isn't it a dandy, Jim? I hunted all over town to find it. You'll have to look at the time a hundred times a day now. Give me your watch. I want to see how it looks on it."

Instead of obeying, Jim tumbled down on the couch and put his hands under the back of his head and smiled.

"Dell," said he, "let's put our Christmas presents away and keep 'em a while. They're too nice to use just at present. I sold the watch to get the money to buy your combs. And now suppose you put the chops on."

The magi, as you know, were wise men—wonderfully wise men—who brought gifts to the Babe in the manger. They invented the art of giving Christmas presents. Being wise, their gifts were no doubt wise ones, possibly bearing the privilege of exchange in case of duplication. And here I have lamely related to you the uneventful chronicle of two foolish

children in a flat who most unwisely sacrificed for each other the greatest treasures of their house. But in a last word to the wise of these days let it be said that of all who give gifts these two were the wisest. Of all who give and receive gifts, such as they are wisest. Everywhere they are wisest. They are the magi.